Table of Content

All That You Need to Know About Tumblr Blogs

-k.koushik

Introduction

Hi, thank you for purchasing this book. In this book, I am going to teach you how to create a tumblr blog. Optimize it, promote it and use it to build your brand or business. Tumblr is a blogging platform like blogger and wordpress.com. Tumblr is also free and anyone can sign up and create a blog.

Creating a tumblr blog has many advantages which I will explain in different parts of this book. Creating a tumblr blog is very easy. You don't need any knowledge of coding or website design. You can customize the blog add pieces of code if you want to (I will show you how to do that too)

One of the biggest advantages of tumblr is that it has a good network and following. You can use it to build your fan base, customers or your own tribe. Using a tumblr blog, you can rank your website easily, send traffic to it.

At the end of every chapter, there will be an activity given. If you follow the activity, following the book will be very easy to you

Happy reading

Advantages of tumblr

Free and easy

Managing and maintaining blogs doesn't require any special knowledge of programming or design.

SEO

Tumblr blogs has many in built SEO benefits one of which is the tags, tumblr has good authority in Google and you will also get its benefits. Use of tumblr for building quality links is also very effective.

Tumblr is also a social media platform

In addition to being a CMS, tumblr is also a social media platform where you can interact with people, follow them, private message them and discuss with them.

Discovery

You can be easily discovered in search engines and it is very useful to build your brand. There is also a big group of audience (who are readers and other bloggers using tumblr) who use the tumblr's search engine to find interesting content.

Backlinks

The main feature which is highly useful in gaining backlinks is reblogging. When your post is reblogged you get a link to your main blog or your website. (Which ever link you give in content source)

Connections

Building friends and followers help you in personally connecting with your customers or readers. This helps you to gain more credibility and trust.

Easy testing of content

If you are trying out a new topic or new way of presentation, you can use tumblr to check whether your content is liked by your readers, by the number of likes, reblogs.

Good for micro blogging

I feel this platform is even better than twitter when it comes to micro blogging. You can post snippets of content in audio, video or graphical formats or text. You don't have to write pages of content to grab your reader's attention because the tumblr community always welcomes and encourages short content. In fact the community prefers short content, especially image or video content (gif animations)

Activity: visit tumblr.com, explore it read different blogs and see what features it has got.

Creating Your Account

Go to www.tumblr.com[1]

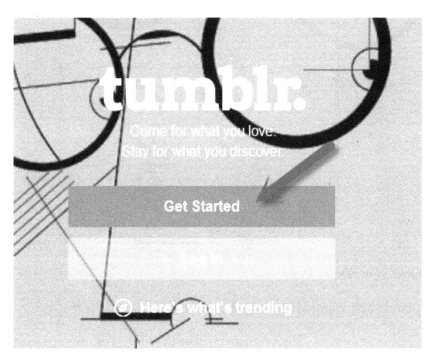

Click get started

---

1. http://www.tumblr.com

Enter your email address

Choose a password for your tumblr account

Choose a username. This username will be the address of your first blog on tumblr.

Your blog's address will be http://username.tumblr.com

You cannot change this address later (it will be the address of your primary blog)

You can also create an unlimited number of blogs in tumblr (if you want) I have tried creating more than 25 blogs in a single account.

After filling the form, click sign up.

Enter your age, click and agree the terms and conditions checkbox, click done.

Login to your email account and click the link sent by tumblr to confirm your registration

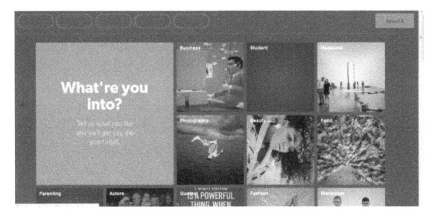

You will be seeing the above screen, choose all the topics you have interest in by clicking the images

I suggest that you select topics relevant to your blog's topic

Then after selecting your interests click next

Your dashboard will be created in a few seconds

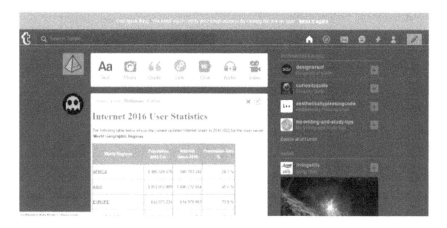

This is how your dashboard will look

Activity: create your account in tumblr.

Changing the appearance of the blog

There are two ways for editing your appearance, the first way is

Click your blog icon and then click edit appearance

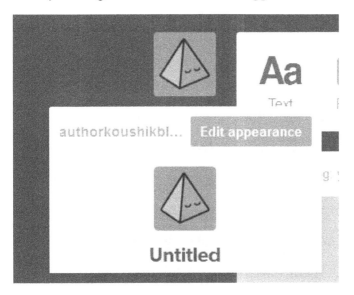

Note: the editing options of the default theme are discussed below. There may be a slight change in the options available depending on your theme. I will show you how to change the theme later in this chapter.

Header

Click on the pencil icon in the top right corner of the header image

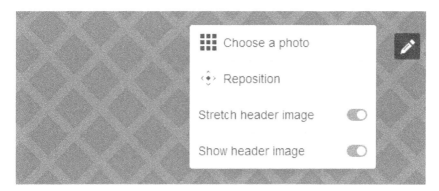

1. Click choose a photo and upload a photo from your PC

2. Now drag the position scrollbar and adjust the position then click done.

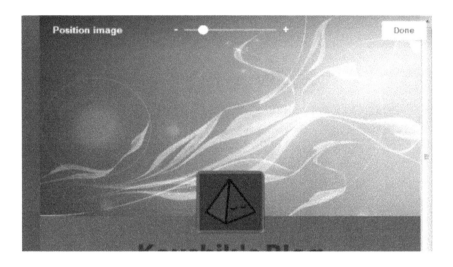

Click save and wait for a few seconds.

Avatar

Click choose a photo and upload an avatar.

If you want to hide the avatar, click the toggle button

Click the circle or square shape to change the shape of the avatar.

Title

Untitled

Just click on the title text (which is Untitled by default)

Delete it and type any title you want

You can also select the title. Change the font and color

You can also hide the title by clicking the toggle button.

Just click anywhere outside after selecting the color and font.

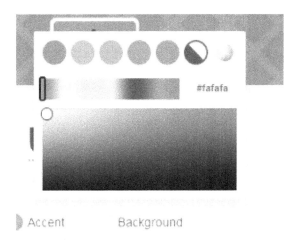

Accent   Background

Click background and change the color.

Note: you can have different themes for different blogs and can change the appearance of each blog uniquely.

Another way of accessing the options of change appearance is

Click my account and then click edit appearance

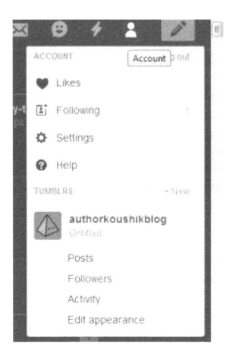

Activity: upload your own avatar, Give your blog a good title and play with fonts and colors.

Setting up your blog

Click account icon, then click settings

Account

Account

Email
writetokoushik@yahoo.com

Let people find your blogs through this address.

Password
·········

Security
Email me about account activity
You will receive an email when someone logs into your account, your password is changed, or a new app is authorized.

Two-factor authentication
Enabling two-factor authentication makes it extra difficult for anyone other than you to access your account. Learn more

Dial-a-post
Set up your phone — This is the '90s. You can call in an audio post from your phone.

Language
English ∨

Active Sessions
Past 30 days

Browser	Location	Last seen
Firefox 49	TN-Chennai, IN	Current session
Windows 7	117.241.75.169	

Delete account

Email

Under **email**, you can change your email address click the pencil icon, (this is the email address you will be using to login to your tumbler account

Let people find your blogs through this address toggle button is on by default. When a toggle button is on it is blue in color and when it is switched off it turns grey.

Password

You can edit the password by clicking the pencil icon, then enter your current password, and new password, then click save.

Security

Under security heading there is Email me about account activity which is switched off by default, you can switch it on so every time your account is accessed you will be sent an email.

You can also activate the two factor authentication if you want. But I don't think it's compulsory.

Dial a post

This is a good feature; it helps you post to your blog from your phone number.

Dial-a-post

Post from

United States ⌄

+1 Mobile number   4-digit pin

Must send Caller ID   Optional

Post to

Koushik's Blog ⌄

Cancel   Save

Enter your number and select which blog to post.

Language English ⌄

Active Sessions
Past 30 days

Browser	Location	Last seen
Firefox 51	TN-Chennai, IN	Current session
Windows 7	117.193.208.136	

Delete account

Language: select your blogs' language, the default is English.

You can see your recent activities log.

Delete account button is to delete your tumblr account permanently. Think twice before using it.

The next settings is dashboard

Dashboard

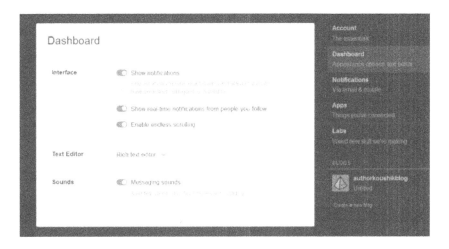

Leave all the settings as default in dashboard

Interface

Under interface

1. Show notifications

2. Find out when you have new followers and when your posts have been liked, reblogged, or replied to.

3. Show real-time notifications from people you follow

4. Enable endless scrolling

All the above options are switched on by default

Text editor you can change your text editor to rich text, HTML or Mark Down (will tell you the differences and usages in next chapter)

Sounds: enable or disable sounds for messages

Notifications

Click the pencil icon near the blog for which you want to change notifications. (All your blogs will be listed here. currently I have only one blog which is showing in the above screenshot)

Switch on or off the notifications and change what you need to be notified of.

Also select from whom you want to receive notifications

Then click save.

Tumblr News

Switch on or turn off tumblr news by clicking the toggle button

Apps

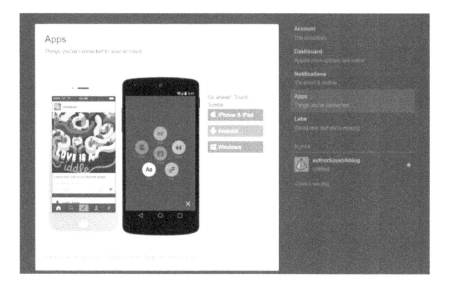

Download the tumblr app for your mobile.

Labs

T U M B L R
LABS

Watch your step　　　□ Enable Tumblr Labs

Experiments

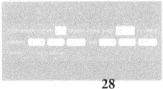

Click enable labs toggle button and start using the various experimental features of tumblr

Blog settings

Click settings and in the right side menu, under the heading blogs, all the blogs you have created will be listed.

Click the blog's name and you will see the settings page of that particular blog

Username

Username is the address of the blog; you can change it anytime you want. But my recommendation is to think well and choose a good keyword rich username. Changing it later affect your SEO benefits. Once you start building backlinks for your blog, promoting your blog. You should not change the username of the blog.

Click pencil icon to edit

Then edit the username.

You can also use a custom domain name for your blog. If you want to use a custom domain name with your blog. You must buy a domain name and have it ready,

Click the use a custom domain toggle button

Enter the domain name which you are going to use.

There are some simple steps you should do to configure your domain to work properly with your tumblr blog.

You need to change your domain's A-record to: **66.6.44.4**

Go to your domain name manager and add an A record to that particular domain name you want to link with your tumblr blog

Click save.

If you want to know more about buying domains, you can read **All That You Need to Know When Buying Domains** https://www.amazon.com/ That-Need-Know-Buying-Domains-ebook/dp/B01NA6NMPS

Then click test domain after configuring correctly , it may take a few hours (24-78 hours) for your domain to be connected to your tumblr blog.

Using a custom domain is completely optional and in my opinion a normal tumblr blog address is enough

Website theme

Editing the theme

You can click Edit theme button to edit theme options or to change your theme.

Click edit theme and wait for a few seconds.

The above screen will be displayed. You can change the appearance options here. Many of the options are similar to edit appearance options which we discussed before.

Scroll down a little bit to see the theme options

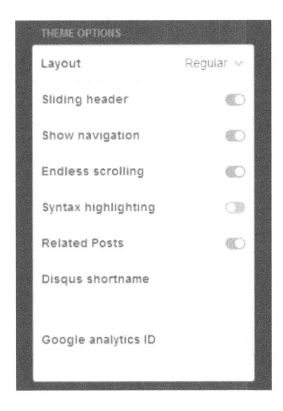

Layout has three choices in dropdown, Regular, Narrow and Grid. This option controls how your posts are arranged in your blog.

Show navigation: is switched on by default, it shows links of all pages of your blog on the top

Endless scrolling: enabled by default, and helps your visitors scroll endlessly to view your posts.

Related posts: shows related posts below your posts.

Disqus shortname: enter your disqus shortname here, if you want to setup a disqus comment system for your tumblr blog.

You should sign up in this site *https://disqus.com and create your shortname.*

Google analytics id: add your Google analytics id to track visitors of your blog.

Adding pages to your blog

Scroll down and you will see Add a page button

Click add a page to add pages to your blog.

You will see the below screen

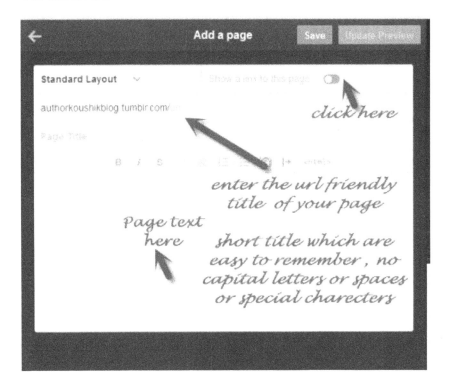

Click show a link to this page toggle button and enable it.

Enter the desired URL of your page

Enter a page title (enter good SEO friendly title)

Type in the title and the text in the text editor

You can also add html by clicking the html button and type in the html code

Click save.

You will be back to the edit appearance page

Scroll down the sidebar till you see advanced options

Click it

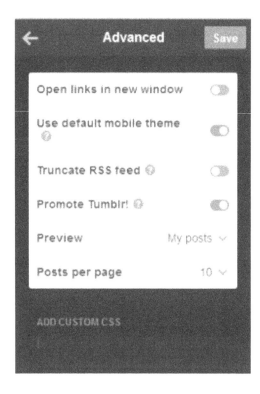

You will see the above options

Click the open links in new window toggle button and enable it.

You can leave all other options as default

You can change the number of posts per page if you need to

You can add any custom CSS code to format or decorate the pages.

Click save

Click back arrow and then click save and click exit

Edit your theme's HTML code

The next option is edit HTML

Click edit html to view and edit the html code of the selected theme.

Edit the html of your theme or add more code. Then click update preview to see the changes.

This is a powerful tool. You can use it really well if you know coding. If you don't know to code, please don't mess with it.

```
<!DOCTYPE html>
<!--[if IE 8]><html class="lt-ie9 lt-ie9"> <![endif]-->
<!--[if IE 9]><html class="lt-ie9"> <![endif]-->
<!--[if gt IE 9]><!--> <html> <!--<![endif]-->
    <head>
        {MobileAppHeaders}
        <meta charset="utf-8">
        <title>{Title}{block:SearchPage} ({lang:Search results for SearchQue
ry}){/block:SearchPage}{block:PermalinkPage}{block:PostSummary} - {PostSumma
ry}{/block:PostSummary}{/block:Per...
        {block:Descr
        <meta name="d                  These options will be applied to your      tion)">
        {/block:Desc                   appearance in the Tumblr dashboard
                                        and apps.
        {block:Hidden}
        <meta name="if:Sliding header" content="1">
        <meta name="if:Show navigation" content="1">
        <meta name="if:Endless scrolling" content="1">
        <meta name="if:Syntax highlighting" content="e">
        <meta name="select:Layout" content="regular" title="Regular">
        <meta name="select:Layout" content="narrow" title="Narrow">
        <meta name="select:Layout" content="grid" title="Grid">
        <meta name="if:Related Posts" content="1">
        <meta name="text:Disqus shortname" content="">
        <meta name="text:Google analytics ID" content="">
        {/block:Hidden}

        <meta name="viewport" content="width=device-width, initial-scale=1.0
, maximum-scale=1.0, user-scalable=no">
        <meta name="theme-color" content="#364650">
        <link rel="shortcut icon" href="{Favicon}">
        <link rel="apple-touch-icon-precomposed" href="{PortraitURL-128}">
        <link rel="alternate" type="application/rss+xml" href="{RSS}">

        <link rel="stylesheet" href="http://static.tumblr.com/gexbavb
/ZpSodrpj0/main-min.css">
        {block:IfSyntaxhighlighting}
        <link rel="stylesheet" href="http://static.tumblr.com/ehmitdz
/2vwnyesih/tumblr-highlightjs.css">
        {/block:IfSyntaxhighlighting}

        <!-- HTML5 Shiv -->
        <!--[if lt IE 9]>
            <script src="http://static.tumblr.com/hriofhd/Qjdm8pn7q/html5shi
v.js"></script>
        <![endif]-->

        <style>
            /* Colors */
```
```
My
```
Hi ever
already

Thank

whit

Changing your theme

Click browse themes

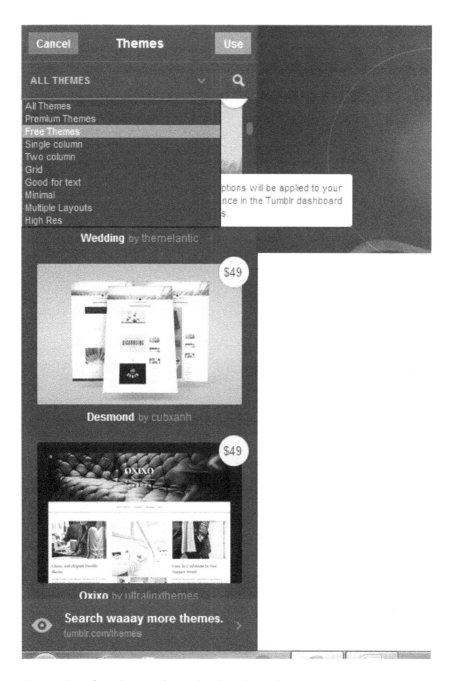

Then select free themes from the dropdown box.

If you want you can spend money on themes but you can do that later on. I have always used free themes and it works fine too.

Then scroll up to see the different themes, click on the themes preview picture to see the preview

If you like the preview of the selected theme, click use. Then click save, then click exit.

If you want to search for more themes, you can click search waay more themes and find more themes there.

Installing custom third-party themes

You can find many themes online offered by third parties for free and for a price.

You can search on Google to find many free themes which are offered by third parties.

But for installing those themes the method is slightly different.

Caution: The problem with third party themes is that you have to manually check whether the theme is updated and then install that theme whenever it is updated. If you are okay with it then you can go for a third party theme.

Advantages of third party themes are: you can stand out of the crowd. Because all the inbuilt themes are commonly used by all the tumblrs. If you can find a unique custom theme online you have the advantage of standing out.

http://zen-themes.com/free-tumblr-themes/alumia/

For the purpose of teaching let me use the theme in the above link

Go to that link, scroll down and click install alumia button

Click somewhere in the text

Then press CTRL+A to select all

Then CTRL+C to copy

Now login to tumblr

Click account icon then click edit appearance of the blog for which you want to install this theme

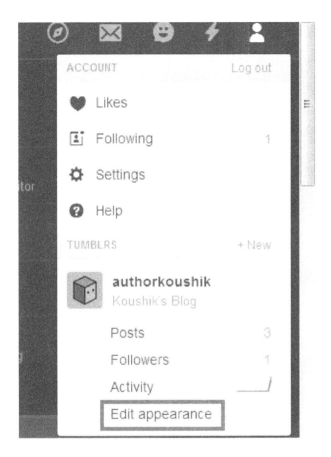

Then click edit theme button

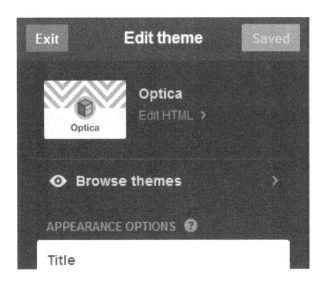

Then click edit html

```
                    "{lang:This far-out Tumblr doesnt follow anyone}",
                    "{lang:This fiercely independent Tumblr doesnt follow
anyone}",
                    "{lang:This Tumblr doesnt follow anything except for its
own rules}",
                    "{lang:This Tumblr doesnt really follow anything}"
            ];
        </script>
        <script src="//ajax.googleapis.com/ajax/libs/jquery/1.9.1/jquery
.min.js"></script>
        <script>!window.jQuery && document.write(unescape('%3Cscript src
="http://static.tumblr.com/vr9xgox/sBgmmjhyw/jquery-1.9.1.min.js"%3E%3C
/script%3E'));</script>
        <script src="http://static.tumblr.com/pdsdtrd/UUvofevpi/main-min
.js"></script>

        {block:IfGoogleAnalyticsID}
            <script>
                (function(i,s,o,g,r,a,m){i['GoogleAnalyticsObject']=r;i[r]
=i[r]||function(){
                (i[r].q=i[r].q||[]).push(arguments)},i[r].l=1*new Date();a
=s.createElement(o),
                m=s.getElementsByTagName(o)[0];a.async=1;a.src=g;m.parentNo
de.insertBefore(a,m)
                })(window,document,'script','//www.google-analytics.com
/analytics.js','ga');
                ga('create', '{text:Google Analytics ID}', 'auto');
                ga('send', 'pageview');
            </script>
        {/block:IfGoogleAnalyticsID}

        {block:IfRelatedPosts}
            {block:RelatedPosts}
                <script src="https://secure.static.tumblr.com/t1owtkf
/bSAnvrou1/jquery.waypoints.min.js" type="text/javascript"></script>
                <script type="text/javascript">
                    $(function() {
                        var trackingPixels = {TrackingPixels};

                        var analytics_frame = document.getElementById
('ga_target');

                        var analytics_iframe_loaded;
                        var eventMethod = window.addEventListener ?
"addEventListener" : "attachEvent";
                        var eventer = window[eventMethod];
                        var messageEvent = eventMethod == "attachEvent" ?
```

Click somewhere in the code. Press CTRL+A then press DELETE key. Then press CTRL+V to paste the code you already copied.

Now you click update preview

Wait for a while then click save

Then click the back arrow button and then click exit to come out of edit theme screen.

Now you can see the new theme installed in your blog.

Encryption

Encryption  Always serve blog over SSL

Serving your Tumblr over SSL helps protect visitors from snoopers and ne'er do wells, but if you've modified your theme it might cause problems. Try it, and if it makes your Tumblr look funny, just come back and disable it.

The toggle button is off by default. You can leave it off usually you need encryption only for ecommerce websites.

Likes

Likes   ⬤◯ Share posts you like

Make your likes public at: tumblr.com/liked
/by/authorkoushikblog

The option for sharing the posts you like to other tumblrs and visitors is on by default you can switch it off if you prefer not to share.

Following

Share the blogs you are following is on by default. I don't recommend you to change it. As you follow more related blogs and share what you are following too. It helps in building traffic. I will discuss in detail in a later chapter.

Replies

Replies	Everyone can reply ⌄
	Everyone can reply
	Tumblrs you follow and Tumblrs following you for a week can reply
Ask	Only Tumblrs you follow can reply

Everyone can reply is the default. That is good too. Only if you get a lot of spam comments in a blog you may have to restrict it.

Ask

Ask   ⬭ Let people ask questions

Send your audience to /ask to ask you questions

This is switched off by default. If you want to build your brand, make your blog interactive and gain trust from your readers. I would recommend you to switch it on. I have explained this in detail in a separate heading

Submissions

Whether you want people to submit posts to your blog or not depends upon what type of blog you are running and also the purpose of your blog.

The posts will be published only after you approve so don't be afraid to try it. It can be beneficial too.

Messaging

Only allow messages from tumblrs you follow is switched off by default. If you receive a lot of unwanted messages, you can switch it on any time you want. Messaging is one of the biggest powers of social platforms so don't disable it unless really necessary.

Advertising

Advertising   On-blog advertising

Allow ads on your Tumblr. Learn more

This is very new to tumblr and they are still figuring out how you will get paid and what is your revenue share. So you can switch it off for now.

Affiliate links

Affiliate links   Change unaffiliated links into Tumblr affiliate links

If you use your own affiliate code, we'll leave your links alone.

Changing unaffiliated links to tumblr affiliate links. I usually switch it off. I always decide whether to use an affiliate link or not to use manually.

Queue

Queue

Automatically publish a queued post
2 times a day ∨ **between** 12 am ∨ **and** 12 am ∨

The queue lets you stagger posts over a period of hours or days. It's an
easy way to keep your blog active and consistent

When you set your posts to queue, the posts are posted in the time you
set here.

Facebook

Click share on facebook a new popup window will open. Click continue as <your name> button.

Then click continue and then click ok

Your account will be shown in your setting s page

All the three toggle buttons are on by default.

You can disable them if needed.

Click the down arrow near the facebook logo to post your posts to any of your pages

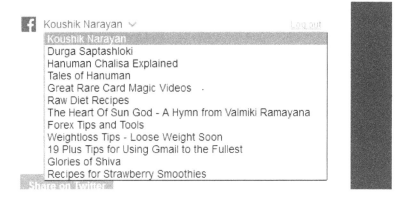

You can logout any time and change to a different account.

Twitter

Click the twitter button and a new tab will open where you have to login to your twitter account and click Authorize app.

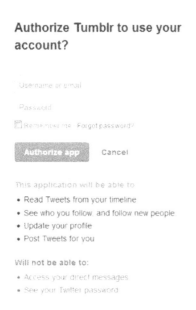

Authorize Tumblr to use your account?

 Cancel

This application will be able to:

- Read Tweets from your timeline
- See who you follow, and follow new people
- Update your profile
- Post Tweets for you

Will not be able to:

- Access your direct messages
- See your Twitter password

Tumblr
By Tumblr, Inc.
www.tumblr.com

The easiest way to blog.

Click authorize app again

Twitter   animationeasy   Log out

You can see your account name on settings page.

Language

Language   English ⌄
                  The language used on your blog.

Language is English by default. You can also create blogs in other languages in tumblr.

Time zone

Timezone   (GMT -5:00) Eastern Time (US & Canada) ⌄

Change your time zone as you prefer. Best option is to use the time zone of your target audience.

Privacy

Allow logged out users to see this blog is on by default. It means your blog is viewable by anyone in the internet and they don't need a tumblr account to view your blog.

Allow the blog to appear in search results is also on by default. You can click the toggle button to disable it if you want to run a secret blog you can share the blogs address (URL) to a number of people whom you want to.

Flag this blog as adult content

Blocked Tumblrs

Blocked Tumblrs   Tumblr to block   Block

Click the pencil button near blocked tumblrs heading.

Enter the username of the tumblr whom you wish to block and then click block.

Delete account button can be used to delete your entire tumblr account

Create new blog

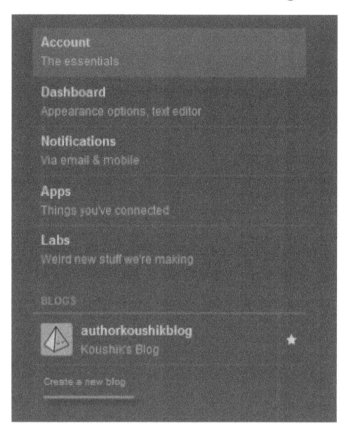

You can see a create a new blog link below the heading Blogs

A new box will popup

Enter the title and URL of your new blog

You can also password protect your blog if you want. Usually you should not. You want your blog to be read by everyone. Right?

Click I am not a robot checkbox and complete the test

Click Create blog button

Your new blog will be created

All your blogs will be listed here under blogs.

You can click the blog's name and you can change the options of your blog.

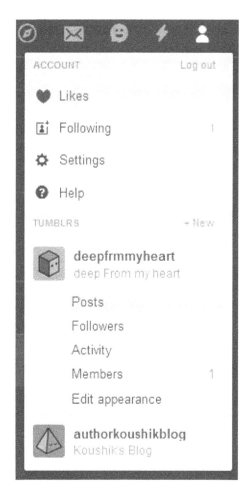

Click account icon and you will see your blogs listed.

Activity:

1. Change the theme of your blog, play around with all the settings and make your blog unique.

2. Connect your facebook page with your blog and automate the posting of your blog posts in facebook

3. Create a new blog and customize it in a different way, using a different theme and by changing the settings.

Start posting

You can post seven different types of content in your tumblr blogs

Text

Let's start posting content now starting from text content

Click the text button

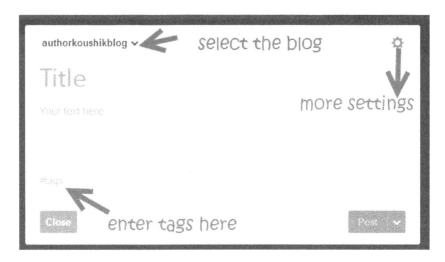

This is your text editor. The important parts of the text editor are labeled in the above image

First dropdown in the menu is the name of your blog.

When you have multiple blogs, you can choose which blog you want to post by clicking the dropdown menu.

Enter the title of the blog post in the title field. Optimizing your post title with relevant keywords would be great for ranking your post. We will discuss about it later

By clicking more settings you can change the URL of the blog post etc

In the **custom URL** field, type the URL friendly title of your blog post

For example if the title is my first Blog post, the URL friendly title can be MyFirstPost. This custom URL is a very useful featured in terms of SEO. Keyword rich URLS are easy to rank in search engines.

Content source is where you should enter the URL of the original content this is automatically filled when you are re-blogging a post. If it is your unique content, then you put the URL of your blog. (Very helpful to build more backlinks)

Post date by default it shows now and it means the current date. You can change it to any date in the past or future. When you enter a future date, the post is scheduled.

Text editor dropdown has 3 options Rich text HTML and Markdown. Rich Text being the default (this can be changed using the blog settings)

You know what is rich text and HTML. Rich text editor is a WYSIWYG editor used to format text without the need to code. When you format it using this editor, the code will be adding automatically in the background.

HTML is where you format your text manually using HTML tags, you can add powerful elements like contact forms using this feature. This is also used when you want to embed something in your blog post.

Markdown: Markdown lets you write using an easy-to-read, easy-to-write plain text format that cleanly converts to valid HTML for publishing on the web. To read more about markdown click the link below

http://daringfireball.net/projects/markdown/

Tags are the place where you should add SEO keywords. Tags are helpful for your visitors to find your posts. Tags are also very useful for you to organize your posts into categories.

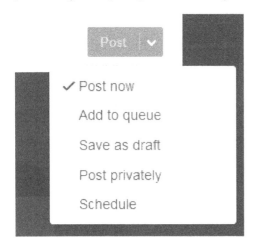

Post dropdown has 5 options, post now being default.

Post now: posts the blog posts immediately.

Add to queue: scheduling the posts in a queue. When the posts in a queue will be scheduled to a particular time and it can be changed through the blogs setting pages

Save as draft: saves the blog post as draft

Post privately: the post will be posted privately (i.e.) that is it will not be visible in your blog.

Schedule: schedule a post to be posted on a future date

Now it's time to type the main text

Click on your text here

You can start typing your post content.

I have typed some sample text. See below

If you click the cursor on the text area you can see small icons appearing on the right side.

It will disappear as you start typing the text.

After finishing your text content, if you press enter you will see those icons again.

Those icons are for adding different types of content within the text post

This means you can press enter between any two lines and add those content elements

Let me explain you the different icons now

Image: for adding images from web or from your device

Video: add video URL or embed code or upload video

Gif: to insert any GIF animation available or upload a GIF

Horizontal line: insert a horizontal line separator

Read more link: display the blog post s an excerpt with a read more link.

Select the text you have typed and some new icons appear

Those icons are for formatting the selected text

Bold · Headline · Strikeout · Unordered list · Italic · Link · Ordered list · Block quote

These formatting options has their own shortcuts too

Bold: CTRL + B

Italic: CTRL + I

Headline: CTRL + shift + 2

Link: CTRL + k

Strikeout: CTRL + SHIFT + 6

Ordered list: CTRL + SHIFT + 7

Unordered list: CTRL + SHIFT + 8

Block Quote: CTRL + SHIFT + 9

Photo

Click upload photos

A file upload dialog box will open

Select the image file you want to upload and click open

Now you can add description tags as usual. You can add all the elements you can to a text type in the description area.

Quote

Add the quote in between the double quotes after deleting the word quote.

Then add the source. Source is the name of the person or the book or any reference you are taking.

You can add the other details in the text area below.

Link

Add the link you want to share in the text box

The description of the link and the image associated with the link is automatically added

You can edit it if you want

The text is plain text so formatting cannot be added

You can add a few carriage returns (Enter key) and spaces to make it look better

You can also cut the summary and paste it in the text area below to format it.

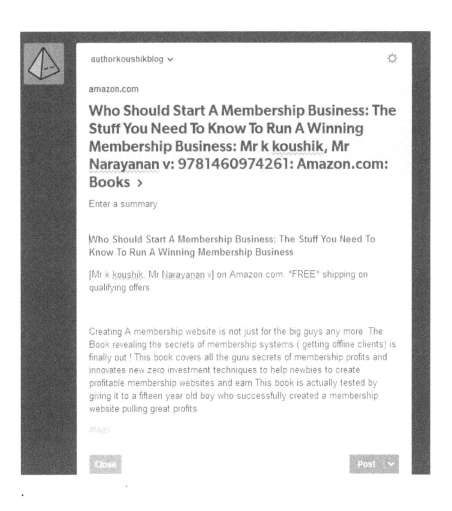

You can also cut short the summary and type your own text or an article related to the link in the text area.

Audio

Enter a web link from sound cloud or a similar service. Or click the headphone icon and upload an Mp3

You will see the above screen. The text area is similar to other content types.

Video

Click add video from web and add a YouTube link or a video sharing websites link

You can paste the embed code

After you paste the YouTube URL, the screen shows the video's preview image.

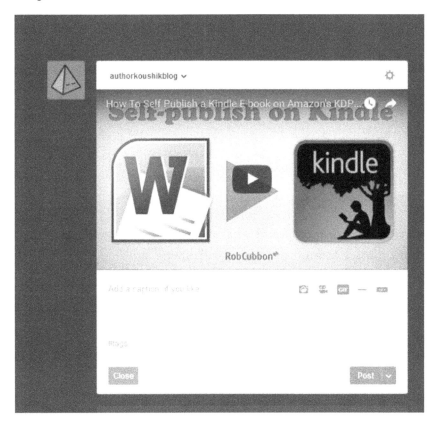

Activity:

1. Create different types of posts.

2. Schedule some posts and add some posts to queue.

3. Try using shortcuts to format text.

What to Post

Now that you know what type of content you can post on tumblr and how to post it. Let me put my views on what kind of posts are the best for this blogging platform.

First you have to decide what you are going to use your blog for.

1. for building a personal blog

2. for building a business blog

3. for building your brand

According to your choice of what you will be doing with your blog, your approach towards the readers will differ.

Personal blog:

If it's your personal blog, you can write all about you, your life and interesting phases. Post your photos, videos, or the things you like. It is very similar to how you use your social network. (Your personal facebook account or twitter account for example.

Your tumblr posts can be shared, or reblogged and replied. This is how your blog post's popularity gets increased and gets viewed by lot of people of the tumblr community.

Though it is your personal blog, please keep in mind that you have to post only interesting content so that it will be shared, you will get replies and even reblogs.

Business blog

If you're having a business blog, please post content which are related to your business, or which helps in building your business. Of course add a personal touch to it but keep it business related. The content should be presented in an interesting way, please give value in the content so it will be shared and reblogged.

As already mentioned, tumblr is a blogging platform and also a kind of social media. So direct advertising or promotion of your business will not work at all. Remember this is a blog and not your business website advertising your products are services directly.

The life of the blog lies in its content. Keep it interesting and info-taining.

You can even write about yourself, the problems you face, etc but completely business related.

You can post your best product reviews, write about your happy customers, how did your product or service bring light to them etc. Your customer relation and support stories, your personal review of the product explaining its advantages, Usage tips, trouble shooting tips and information about the product. Overview of the products etc

Building your brand

By the word building your brand, what I mean now is making yourself established as an authority or a professional. Like Author, musician, Web designer or a celebrity in your field. Now this is slightly different from your business blogs, the keen difference between business blog and this one is that this is person centric.

Let me take an example of an author to explain you the concept.

For example an author should not only promote his books but also build a loyal fan base who not only likes his books but also the author himself. This blog will be a mixture of personal stuff and profession related stuff, profession related content being higher. You can write how you feel as an author, why did you write your book. Why do you like your book? Conversations with your fans, the support and appreciation you got. Your best book reviews, the events you are participating in as an author. About your best fan letters,

You will also write about your books, book reviews, book launches, giving free review copies and other stuff but you will also introduce yourself to your readers, interact with them and share your feelings, memories etc.

This way your fans will get to know you. They will not only love your books but also love you.

This way they will start trusting you and will read your books for the fact that you are its author. Like fans of actors going to watch movies just because their favorite actor stars in the movie. That is, they completely trust that if their favorite actor is starring, they would love the movie.

Five golden rules of blogging in tumblr:

1. **Never stick to a single type of content**, post audios, videos, text, web links, and chats, utilize all the types of content to keep it interesting.

2. **Blog regularly**, have a fixed day, once a week or once or twice a month. And schedule your posts to be published on that date; your readers should know when you will post. Blogs which don't have regular content gets no visitors. (Even though the content is interesting) a blog always needs a flow of content.

3. **Keep the text short**; use a lot of attractive images

4. **never use low quality videos or images**. It ruins everything. Design your images carefully. You can always use a good image or video from the internet and give credits to the source. That's the best to do in tumblr.

5. **Find related content** for your blog and reblog it or share links from other websites

Some extra important things to be remembered

Don't hesitate or be shy to ask for a reblog or a share. Request them to reblog and share your posts and also explain them in short why reblogging your content would be useful.

Ask them to follow you if they like your posts.

Have a call of action or an activity for your readers if possible, because interactive blogs get more response. The call of action may be a simple comment of their opinion or visiting a website link with related content and a recommendation to buy a book. Call of action works, it shows that you are serious and trust worthy.

Concentrate on tags. Do you know your followers can follow specific tags by tracking them? Yes they can. Add keyword rich, meaningful, easy to find and relevant tags to your post (I know I already talked about this to you but I am reminding you as it is important.

Catch up with the trend

Best way to get more reblogs and likes and followers is to post in the topics which are searched for. You can explore the current trends of tumblr by following the link below

https://www.tumblr.com/explore/trending

You can scroll down and see some of the posts and click on them if they are related to your niche to some extent. Look at the tags and note them down,

You can also see the staff picks and

You can access the same page by clicking the explore button.

SEO for Tumblr

Though having a tumblr blog has its own SEO benefits as it is a famous blogging platform and social site ranked in search engines, you should do some search engine optimization both on on-page and off-page

On page SEO includes

Title:

Choosing a catchy keyword optimized title for every blog post and using the URL friendly version of your blog title for the URL. Use the main related keyword which is the main keyword in the content in the title. Be creative with the title and use keywords only where it makes sense (i.e.) don't artificially stuff keywords in your title.

Content

Use the correct keywords within the content. Use the keywords 2 or 3 times within the first 125 words if possible. If the content is less than 300 words, just use the keywords once per keyword or twice. Be creative with the opening lines of the content. Write it and structure it in a way that your readers will be interested to read till the end,

Don't use long text articles with tumbler. It doesn't work very well. Use images, info- graphics, videos and links. Keep the text short and sweet. Don't promote anything directly. Give free content and recommend the product if it is related to the content you are writing.

Example: if you are promoting a blender, write a few recipes which use the blender and recommend the product with a link. Don't stuff your content with links and offers directly.

When you are posting an audio, image, link or video content type, you can use the text area below it to post a transcription of audio or video and a short description for the image content.

Link to related posts and cross link them for good internal linking.

Tags

use, long keywords and also broad keywords. If you are writing about Best SEO keyword research practices for on page SEO, include the keyword SEO, on page SEO, keyword research, keyword analysis, best keyword research, key word research, keyword research tools, keyword analysis tools. Best Tools for SEO may be some of the keywords you can use as tags

What I am insisting is people searching for SEO, keyword analysis, SEO practices and other relevant topics should also be able to find your post.

You can also generate tag based links in tumblr to build backlinks to posts under the same tag. This will give you a good effect.

Activity:

Create some posts following the suggestions and guidelines, test different content types and see which one works out the best for you.

Promoting your Tumblr blog

Now that you have a blog, you need to start promoting it inside and outside of tumblr. Promoting your blog outside of tumblr is just as promoting any other website or blog so I am not covering it here. Tumblr is a big community in itself and you should leverage the traffic which you get from the inside and in my opinion tumblr community is the most interactive and participating community than other blogging communities. The bloggers love searching for content inside tumblr for the purpose of rebloging or for the purpose of reading pleasure, most of the bloggers are good readers too.

Remember the rules about what to post and how to post because only good posts are benefited by promotion.

Following blogs and gaining followers

This is a very important heading. It could have been a separate chapter but I am putting it here for your ease. Followers are like subscribers. If a tumbler follows you then he will see all your posts in his dashboard. Follower is like your blog's fan or at least a regular reader who is interested in your blog's topic and wants to read all the posts from your blog. Your followers are the ones who will probably reblog your posts.

Followers are the most beneficial feature of tumblr and also the most powerful.

Invite your friends to follow your blog

You can send email and facebook messages to your friends and can invite them to follow your blog. This will give you an initial boost of followers.

Follow relevant blogs

Search for blogs relevant to your niche and follow them.

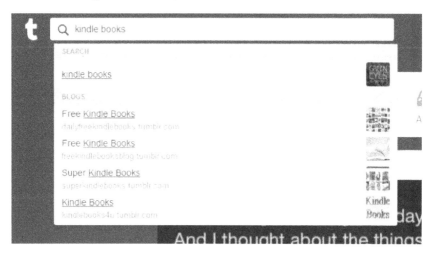

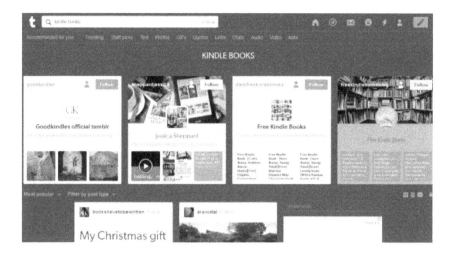

Mostly, most of them you follow will follow you back.

Asking to follow back

After following a number of blogs and waiting for a few days you can message them and ask them nicely and politely to follow you back. Most of the time, people in tumblr follow you when you follow them and ask them to follow you back. This is not going to be as hard as you think.

Ask people to follow your blog in your posts.

Note: use your blog for a while, add useful and interesting content. Follow relevant blogs and after a while you can ask people to follow you. That way you will get a better response. Brand new unverified blogs cannot contact people and their posts take time to be visible in search pages and tag pages.

Clone your popular posts, (i.e.) see which posts are getting likes, shares and notes and try to create more posts like that. You can also repeat popular posts after some good gap (by reworking on it so that it is slightly different and the people don't get bored and un-follow you) but don't overdo it. Remember that your followers will also get new followers by time and when you reblog your popular posts after some time, those new followers of your followers may become your followers too. Use this strategy wisely.

Reblogging popular posts

Search for popular posts in your niche and reblog them to make your blog interesting. Maybe your followers will like and reblog that content from you. You also have a good chance of getting the original posters attention. And he may be interested in your blog and follow you.

Message

Tumblr message is also known as fan mail which is an in built private messaging system of tumblr. You can message to any tumblr blog you follow and you will receive messages from anyone who follows your blog. It is not restrictive and controlled when compared to other social media. I say this because the blog you want to message doesn't have to follow you for you to message them. All it takes to send a message to them is to simply follow them.

Some facts about messages or fan mails

Both your primary and secondary blogs can receive fan mails from followers and it is received in the same inbox,

Only text messages can be sent through messages, no images or other type of content are allowed.

The messages are customizable with templates

There is no limit with the number of messages you can send in a day. Use it wisely and don't over use it.

Posts being reblogged and shared.

Reblogging and sharing are the powers of tumblr blogs, which is how you gain traffic to your blogs and websites.

A tumblr post can be easily shared by clicking the share icon which is found below every post

The share icon is the first icon from the left, the icon which looks like a play button.

By clicking it you can see different options which popup in a box shape. (Shown in the above screenshot)

Readers can grab the link of that particular post by clicking the permalink button.

The embed button gives the embed code which your readers can post in their website or blogs to show your post directly in any page they want.

Clicking the email button asks you to enter recipient emails to email them the link of that post; this makes the work easier for your reader to share this link to themselves or their friends.

The report button is used to report the content of that post if something wrong has been posted (you are certainly not going to though.) But it increases the safety and comfort of your readers. So it is actually good tumblr has one.

Please do not use that unnecessarily.

That is not all. if you hover your mouse pointer, you will see a horizontal scroll bar (shown in the below image)

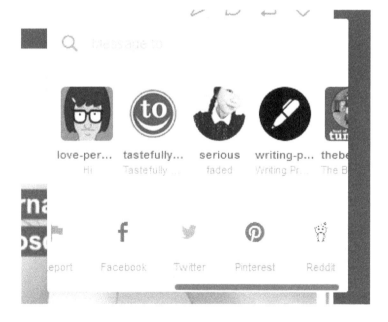

There are options to share the post through facebook, twitter pinterest and reddit

They can also message the post to their tumblr friends using the message to text box or by clicking the avatars of your friends.

Activity:

1. Follow your favorite tumblrs, make friends, communicate with other tumblrs, create notes (comments) in your favorite blog posts and interact with people. Make some friends.

2. Share good blog posts, reblog them. Follow back the persons who follow you.

Ask me anything

Ask me anything is a great feature by tumblr, it helps you to communicate and interact with tumblrs, let me explain you how to enable this feature on your blog. This increases communication because people like to ask questions and when you particularly request them to you will get a lot of questions which increases the number of persons you know in tumblr. You make friends, develop fans or readers.

If you are a how to writer, or a writer in general, you will be getting questions about your writing, sometimes you also get ideas generated for your posts through these questions.

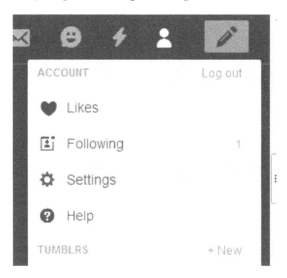

Click the account icon

Click settings

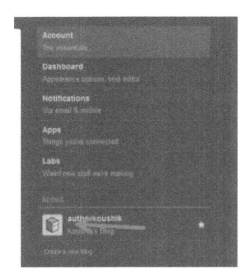

Click the blog for which you want to enable ask me anything

The blog's settings page will be loaded, scroll down to find this

Click the toggle button let people ask questions

If you want you can change the title of that page from ask me anything to something else you prefer.

You can enable allow anonymous questions if you want, I usually don't enable it because I am interested to know who is asking the questions and I believe spam and bad messages are avoided by leaving it disabled.

Visit your blog and now you can find an ask me anything link somewhere depending up on your theme.

Now when someone asks a question you get it in your tumblr inbox (the messages)

Click the mail icon

Click the pencil icon to respond to messages

Type in the answer

Click the plus icon which appears after every return key (enter key) you press to add images, videos, gifs and even read more links (if you want to) just like your normal post

Now you can do two things

You can click answer privately to answer the tumblr in his private message

Or you can post it.

If you click the post button it is publically posted in your blog, with the question asked by the tumblr in the top of your post

Note: after you answered the question the message no longer appears in the messages.

When you answer the question the person who asked the question is notified by email.

You also get an email notification when someone asks a question.

Activity:

1. Create an ask me anything page in your blogs

2. Create a text post or image post to request people to ask you questions.

Monitoring your blog

To see what is happening in your blog, the number of posts, the number of followers you have got at this time, the recent activities related to that blog etc

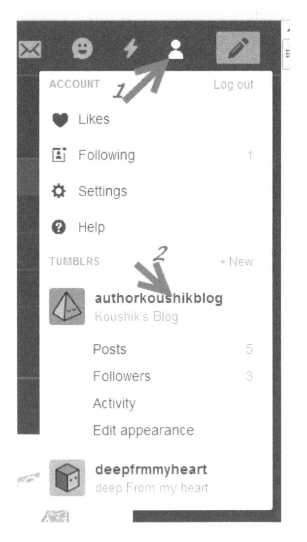

Click the my account icon

Click the blog of which you want to see the details about

You will be taken to the page shown below

You have four menu buttons in the right navigation menu

Posts: showing all the posts posted in that particular blog of yours.

Followers: showing the list of all followers following that particular blog

You can also follow them back by clicking the follow button given near their names

If you are already following them, the follow button will not be visible.

You can also hover over their name and you will get a grey block button, you can block them if you don't want them to follow you. Use it only when it is really necessary.

Note: You can also click the image near their blog name and see a preview what kind of posts they post etc before following them

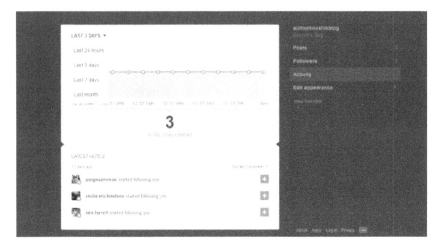

You can change the time frame from the time dropdown

You can see the number of followers, notes (comments), and list of followers within a certain time frame

Edit appearance: is used to change your theme and appearance of the blog and color schemes. Already explained in detail.

Activity: click activity to see all activities related to the blog

Use post editor

this link takes you to the mega post editor

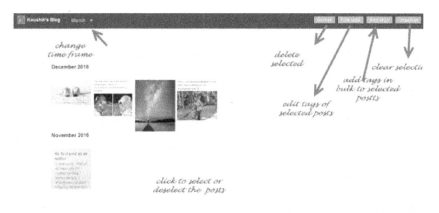

You can change the time frame clicking the dropdown and see the posts that were posted within that time frame,

Click add tags to add new tags to the selected posts, (click the posts to select)

Just type in the tags with commas and then click add tags to add the tag to all selected posts.

Click edit tags to remove the existing tags in bulk from selected posts.

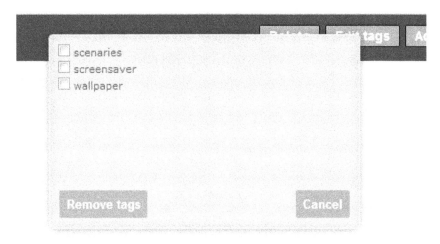

Select the tags you want to remove and click Remove tags button.

Unselect is to clear selection so that you can select a different set of posts again.

Delete is to bulk delete the blog posts

Just close that tab or window after your editing work is over. This helps you a lot in bulk editing or deleting your posts.

Activity:

1. Check the activities regularly.

2. Use mega post editor and add new tags, remove tags which are not relevant.

Setting up your private blog network

What is a private blog network

A **blog network**, also known as a link farm, is a group of **blogs** that are owned by the same entity. A **blog network** can either be a group of loosely connected **blogs**, or a group of **blogs** that are owned by the same company

The definition of a private blog network is a network of many smaller websites; each focused around one specific subject (i.e. niche websites), all ultimately linking back to a single large primary website. It is a means of driving traffic from a targeted audience. These networks often consist of anywhere from 50 to hundreds of websites, and each website on a PBN can be altered at any time to fit the needs of a different primary website. They are typically purchased or re-sold in bulk packages

How to create a Private Blog network in tumblr

Now that you know what a private blog network is, you may have guessed how to create a PBN using tumblr. If not don't worry its easy and simple.

By now you already know that you can create multiple blogs in tumblr and a PBN is a network of blogs which are interlinked. Each blog may be covering a sub topic or sub niche of your main niche. Now all you have to do is create multiple blogs with each blog being a related niche or sub topic of your main business blog.

Click my account icon, you will see a list of blogs you already created under the title tumblers,

Click the +new button

You will be taken to create a new blog screen,

After this step the other steps are all the same.

Some tips to follow when creating a private blog network

Use a different theme for each blog in the network.

Keep the content of the blogs related to each other so it can be interlinked. Also post content related to your main niche in all the blogs once in a while to keep the blogs connected.

If you work in multiple unrelated niches, have separate accounts for each unrelated niches and build a number of blogs related to that particle niche.

You can also invite your friends or co workers or anyone you want to post to your blog. (You cannot invite users to post to your primary blog. Only you can post in your primary blog according to tumblr. Primary blog is the first blog you created using that account.

Secondary blogs are the other blogs created from that account.

The disadvantages of secondary blogs is that Secondary blogs cannot, however, follow other

Blogs, like posts, ask questions to other users, or submit posts to other blogs.

To read more about your primary blog and secondary blogs visit the link below

https://www.tumblr.com/docs/en/blog_management.

Activity:

1. Set up a PBN

2. Promote it. (See tips from the heading promoting your blogs)

Tumblr for building backlinks

Tumblr is a great tool for building back links to your websites, blogs or anything you want to boost the rankings in search engines.

All you need to do is to post something interesting, add a link to your website or product in that post. Also leave a note in the bottom asking people to reblog and share the post if they like it. When they reblog your post, your link is also present in the post gaining back links to your website.

You can also curate contents from your main website and add the link of the original post (from your main website) in content source to generate visitors.

The most reblogged kinds of contents are

Funny images, gifs, and interesting funny contents, quotes, jokes, short stories etc gets reblogged a lot.

Reminder: use your caption area, tags and URL well. Add tags related to your niche, use a SEO friendly URL for your blog post.

Activity:

1. Curate some interesting content from your target website (the website for which you want to drive traffic)

2. Add links in the bottom of the blog post, you can also ask people to visit that website for more related content.

Video marketing using tumblr

You can easily boost the SEO ranking of your videos in YouTube, vimeo and other video sharing websites using your tumblr blogs alone.

Preparing your video

The video should be interesting and nice. The quality of the video should be good. Always give a HD option for your viewers. The video should be very informative or funny and exciting.

The video should be made in such a way the viewers view the video till the end. If the video is not presented well, then the viewers may just stop watching it

Optimize your video's description using good relevant and targeted keywords in it. Use low competitive long tail keywords which are specific to your video. Describe the video nicely (the description should be 150-250 words at the minimum it can be up to 320 words. don't write lengthier descriptions than that.

The filename of the video file you are uploading to YouTube should be the main keyword you are trying to rank the video for.

Make sure that there are lots of thumbs up for your video and only a few thumbs down if any.

Follow the on page SEO tips which we discussed before. Optimize your title, and description, and add relevant keywords too.

Add the video to the right category. Do some research, see how similar videos are categorized.

Now that you have uploaded your video to your YouTube channel, you can start promoting it and start getting more subscribers. I am not covering those techniques

In my opinion, by using the tumblr blog correctly, you can gain traffic, thumbs up and subscribers. So let's start posting your YouTube video to tumblr.

Posting your video to tumblr

You already know how to post a video to your tumblr blog. If not refer the start posting chapter.

Don't directly upload the video to blog, just paste the embed code of your video from YouTube. That will help you in ranking.

Take the description of the video and quickly rewrite it and paste in the video description area in tumblr.

Then post the video.

You can also post your video in multiple tumblr blogs. That will really help in ranking your video

If you follow the SEO tips correctly and your video is interesting and giving value to viewers, your video will be reblogged hundreds of times, and then the video will go viral.

Your video will rank in search engine within a few days.

Activity:

1. Post interesting videos from your YouTube channel in tumbler.

2. Write an interesting captions, also ask people to reblog if they like the video.

Some awesome plugins to ease your work

Tumblr doesn't allow any plugins to be installed like wordpress or other blogging platforms. The plugins that I am talking about are the plugins which you can install to your favorite browsers to improve your user experience and to speed up tumblr related tasks.

Xkit

Reblog yourself. Post your crushes. Block the posts you don't like. Blacklist words. Shorten long posts. Even automatically scroll your dashboard. This is a very useful plugin which works in Firefox, chrome and safari. Xkit is not a single extension but a package of various extensions so you can easily customize it and remove the features which you don't want to use and install them when needed.

You can download it from http://xkit.info/seven/download/

Tumblr post

Lets you post photos, videos, mp3s, quotes and links to your Tumblr blogs using the "Post to my tumbler blog" menu items in the context menu of the content that you want to post or by dragging and dropping it onto the extension's toolbar icon in Firefox. This is just like using a social bookmarking tool, instead of bookmarking you are going to post interesting content you find in internet to your tumblr blogs.

https://addons.mozilla.org/en-us/firefox/addon/tumblr-post/[1]

If you are a chrome user you can use a similar plugin which can be download from the below link

https://chrome.google.com/webstore/detail/post-to-tumblr/ipkpjkniknhaojcebeaallaglkmhlcno

---

Tumblr savior:

This is a good plugin for modifying the tumblr feed you see in your dashboard. You can add words to white list and blacklist the white lists are the tags which you would love to read about and blacklist is the list of topics you don't want to read about, keeping your feed clean for you.

https://chrome.google.com/webstore/detail/tumblr-savior/oefddkjnflmjbclpnnoegglmmdfkidip

Using these plugins, you can easily speed up your task and also make your blogging experience better with tumblr.

Activity:

Try all these different plug-ins.

Automating the blogging process

Now that you know how to create a fully functional tumblr blog, let me cover some of the tips for automating some of the tasks in tumblr so that you can concentrate more on creating new content and marketing your blog.

The best tool to help us in automation is the IFTTT

There is a small disadvantage in automating your blogs using IFTTT. Only one tumblr blog can be connected with your IFTTT ACCOUNT. If you have multiple blogs you need a separate IFTTT account for every blog you want to automate.

But not a big issue right, all you need is a unique email address for each blog Now its action time,

Sign up for an IFTTT account for your blog. (With a new email address you made for your blog)

Go to https://IFTTT.com/

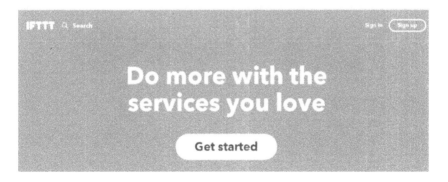

Click sign up

Enter email and password and click sign up

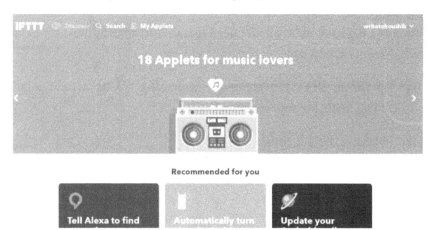

You will be taken to the home page

We are going to automate the posting of different kinds of content to your blog

Image content

We are going to automate it through flicker

Create a separate flicker account for every blog you want to automate.

Click my applets

Click new applet

You will be taken to the page shown below

Click the plus sign near if

You will be taken to the choose a service page.

Choose a service

Q   flick

Want to build even richer Applets?

Search for flickr and click the flickr logo

You will be taken to the connect to flickr page (shown below)

Connect Flickr

Flickr is an image hosting and video hosting website, web services suite, and online community. The service is widely used by bloggers to host images that they embed in blogs and social media

Want to build even richer Applets?

Click connect

A popup will popup asking you to login to flickr

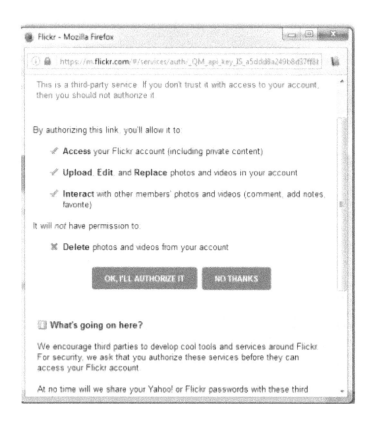

After you login you will be taking to the above page

Click OK, I'LL AUTHORIZE IT button

Then the popup will close and you will be taken to choose trigger page

‹ Back

Choose trigger

Step 2 of 5

You can do a number of things with this.

When you upload new photos,

When you upload a new photo and tag it with a particular tag

Any new photo you upload

When you favorite a public photo

When you create a new set

We are going to click new public favorite.

Favorite is similar to a like, you can favorite any public photos you want to. We are going to use it to automate image posting in tumblr

Click new public favorite

You will be taken to this page

143

Click the plus sign after then

You will be taken to choose action service page.

Choose action service

Step 3 of 6

Q tum

Tumblr

Search for tumblr and click the tumblr logo

The choose action page will appear

Create a text post	**Create a link post**	**Create a photo post**
This Action will create a text post on your Tumblr blog.	This Action will create a link post on your Tumblr blog.	This Action will create a photo post on your Tumblr blog.

Create a quote post	**Create an audio post from URL**	**Create a video post**
This Action will create a quote post on your Tumblr blog.	This Action will create an audio post on your Tumblr blog from the given URL to an MP3 file.	This Action will create a video post on your Tumblr blog from the given URL to a YouTube video, a Vimeo video, a URL to a video file, or an embed code.

Click create a photo post

Complete action fields

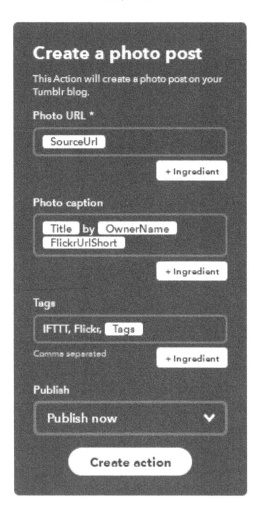

You can now customize the photo caption field by adding a description to it.

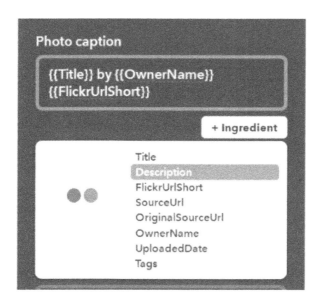

Place the cursor after the last closing brackets and then click +
ingredients and click description to add it

If you don't want to add description you can skip the above step

Now customize your tags by deleting the tags IFTTT, flickr and adding
your own niche keywords

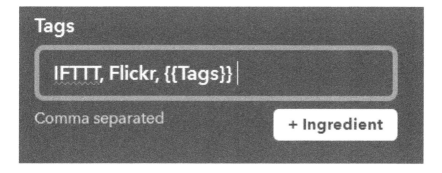

147

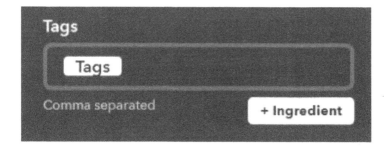

Now you can change the publish options

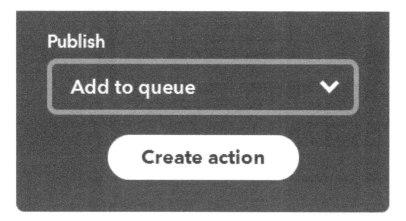

Click create action

Review and finish page will be loaded

Review and finish

Receive notifications
when this Applet runs

Finish

Click the green toggle button and it will turn grey. Do this if you don't want to get email notifications when posts are added

Then click finish

Links from pocket account.

Create a separate pocket account with your email addresses you created for each blog.

You can use it to automate the posting of links to your blogs.

You can sign up for your pocket account by visiting the link below.

https://getpocket.com/

After signing up go to IFTTT.com and login

Click my applets

Then Click new applet

Want to build even richer Applets?

Click the plus sign near if

You will be taken to the choose a service page

Choose a service

Q   pock

Pocket

Want to build even richer Applets?

Search for pocket and click the pocket logo

Connect Pocket

Step 1 of 6

Pocket is a service that lets you save what you find on the web to watch and read on any device, anytime.

Connect

Want to build even richer Applets?

Click connect

A popup window will appear requesting you to log in

Login to the pocket account you created for your blog

After you login successfully another window will pop up

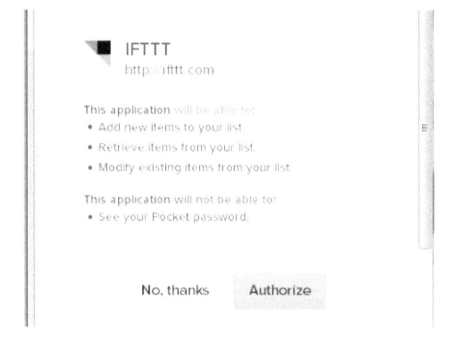

Click authorize

Then the popup window will close

You can see the choose trigger page loaded in your browser (shown below)

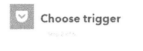

Choose trigger

Step 2 of 6

Click any new item, you can use any of the four triggers to automate the posting using pocket, I am just choosing any new item for demonstration the steps

Click the plus sign after then

You will be taken to choose action service page.

Choose action service

Step 3 of 6

Q   tum

Tumblr

Search for tumblr and click the tumblr logo

The choose action page will appear

Click create a link post

Complete action fields

Create a link post

This Action will create a link post on your Tumblr blog.

Title

> Title

+ Ingredient

Link URL *

> Url

+ Ingredient

Description

> Excerpt via Pocket

+ Ingredient

Tags

> IFTTT, Pocket, Tags

Comma separated

+ Ingredient

155

Publish

Delete the, IFTTT, Pocket in the tags text field

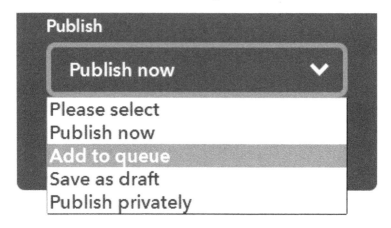

Change the publish combo box to add to queue

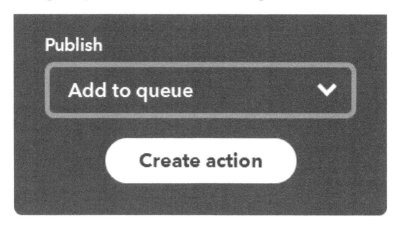

Click create action

Now you will be taken to review and finish page

Review and finish

If any new item added by
animationeasy@gmail.com,
then create a link post on
your Tumblr blog

93/140

by writetokoushik

works with

Receive notifications
when this Applet runs

Finish

Want to build even richer Applets?

Click finish

Your applet is ready to work

If any new item added by animationeasy@gmail.com, then create a link post on your Tumblr blog

by writetokoushik

On

- Created on Jan 23 2017
- Never run

This Applet can be delayed by up to an hour

Check now

works with t

Video content

Click my applets

You don't have any Applets
Applets work with all your favorite services

Get started

New Applet

Click new applet

You will be taken to the page shown below

if ✚ this then that

Want to build even richer Applets?

Click the plus sign near if

Choose a service page will appear (shown below)

Choose a service

Q yout|

YouTube

Want to build even richer Applets?

Search for YouTube and click YouTube logo, then a popup will ask you to login and connect to your YouTube account.

Note: you need a separate YouTube account for every blog for this automation purpose. (You will understand why when we finish the applet). If you don't have a separate YouTube account already make on for each blog you want to automate.

After clicking the YouTube logo you will be taken to the page where it says connect to YouTube

Click the connect button

A window will popup asking you to login to YouTube. After you login you will be taken to the page shown below

Choose trigger

Step 2 of 6

New liked video	New public video from subscriptions	New public video uploaded by you
This Trigger fires every time you like a video on YouTube.	This Trigger fires every time a specific user you are subscribed to makes a new video public.	This Trigger fires every time you upload a new public video to YouTube.

Now you can chose three triggers after connecting to your YouTube account

The triggers are

1. New liked video

2. A new public video uploaded by you

3. New public video from your subscriptions

I feel I have more control when I choose the trigger a new liked video.

Because I will like only the videos I want on my blog from this YouTube account

We don't want all videos from the subscriptions as all cannot be relevant

You can also choose new public video uploaded by you if you upload videos frequently in YouTube which I don't do.

I clicked new liked video

You will be taken to the next screen (shown below)

Click the plus sign near then

Choose action service

Step 3 of 6

Q   tumb

Tumblr

Want to build even richer Applets?

Search for tumbler and click the tumblr logo

Now you will see the screen for selection actions

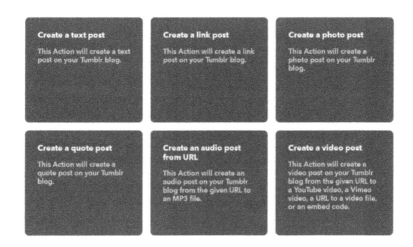

It will show the kind of posts you can create

Click create a video post (as we are going to take content from YouTube

You will see the create a video post page

Now you can customize your post by doing two things

Now customize the caption by deleting the text liked on YouTube

I also like to delete the URL

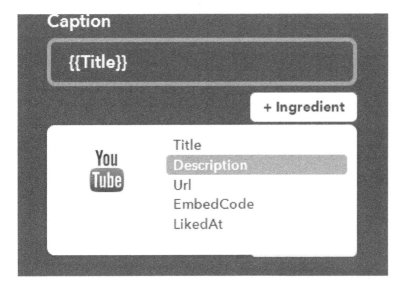

Now place your curser after the '}' sign and click +ingredient and click description to add it

Next thing to do is to customize the tags

Delete the tags IFTTT, YouTube

Add your main niche keywords. You can later bulk edit keywords using the mega post editor

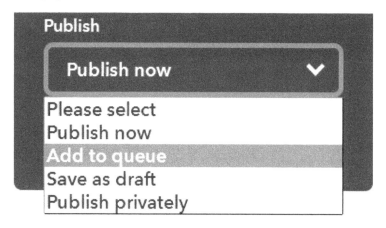

Select add to queue from the publish options, it's always better to add to queue rather than publishing immediately, to maintain the posting time and regularity.

You can like a hundred videos when you are free and then post, 3-5 videos a day depending on your choice.

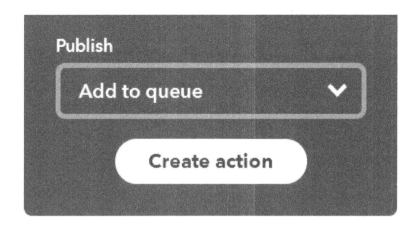

Click create action

Now you will be taken to review and finish page

Review and finish

Receive notifications
when this Applet runs

Finish

Want to build even richer Applets?

It says if new liked video, and then create a video post on your Tumblr blog. That's what we want :)

Click the toggle switch if you don't want to receive email notifications when the applet is running

Click finish

Now you can see your YouTube applet in my applets> YouTube

Applet ID 48362710d

Audio content

You can also automate the posting of audio content to your blog using sound cloud and IFTTT.

Now you know how to create applets. Take this as your exercise and create an applet that automates the posting of audio content to your blog. I am not describing the process as it is very similar to what you have done with YouTube, flicker and pocket account.

Now that you have automated the posting of content to your blog, you can just like the videos, audio clips and favorite the images from flickr. Save links to your pocket account and the posting is taken care by IFTTT.

This method saves you a lot of time and you can work on marketing, promoting your blog, writing unique content etc.

Note: though you have automated the blog posting, you have to be posting some unique hand written content or unique images or videos particularly designed by yourself (your team or your company) because whatever you do, if there is no uniqueness you cannot succeed in building your brand.

Activity:

1. Create an auto-blog. (Though it is semi auto. Let's call it auto)

2. Explore IFTTT to find new ways to automate blog posts.

Placing ads in your blog

With the recent policy changes of tumblr. Which I don't think they have made an official announcement yet. They have banned adsense ads in tumblr. Adsense was one of the most quick and easy monetization methods. Now though the doors of tumblr are closed for adsense ads you can still monetize your blog with a couple of tactics.

I am not coving this in detail because the process is big and different but let me give you some ideas.

1. Promoting your products like tea shirts or other merchandise created through cafepress, zazzle or teespring. This was very popular in early 2016 but still if you put some more effort you can succeed.

2. Selling self published book in your niche through kindle (eBooks) or createspace and lulu (Paperbacks), my opinion is kindle sells more.

3. Promoting affiliate products by writing informative reviews or user guides.

4. Exchange of text link ads for a monthly fee or placing text link ads in your blog for a monthly fee.

You can sign up to one of the market places or all of them and offer your service.

http://www.backlinks.com/

http://www.backlinks4u.com/

http://www.selected-links.com/

There are many similar sites you can find in Google.

Of course digital point forums

Warrior forums

And other internet marketing forums can be good place to search for selling text links too.

Activity:

Monetize your blog, start earning money

Resources

Check this link for knowing about hidden features of tumblr

https://www.tumblr.com/docs/en/lesser_known_features

Did you love *All That You Need to Know About Tumblr Blogs*? Then you should read *Canva Tips and Tricks Beyond The Limits*[1] by Koushik K!

Even for professional designers with training and experience in sophisticated graphic design software packages like corel draw and photoshop, Canva is a quick and easier solution for quality designs with all the ready-made templates, ease of use.For hobby designers or newbies Canva is like a great gift because of its user-friendly, self-explanatory and easy interface.

I once taught Canva a friend who was never inclined towards graphic design and now, he uses it full time to produce graphics for work and personal purposes.

---

1. https://books2read.com/u/mdnqaw

2. https://books2read.com/u/mdnqaw

By that experience, I can say Canva is one of the best web applications out there for producing sophisticated designs easily either for social media or for print. Canva's core advantage is its very little learning curve.

This book will mainly deal with the limitations of Canva and how to deal with them (Legally) without having to pay for it.

Who is this book written for?

Anyone who wants to design quickly and efficiently without much hassle using CanvaAnyone who loves Canva and want to know more about using it efficientlyAnyone who do not wish to buy Canva pro at this time and want to overcome the limitations of Canva (legally)**What will you learn in this book?**

Hidden features of Canva and how to use themCanva tips and tricksCanva secretsWorkarounds for Canva pro only features.Do things you can do only with Canva pro without Canva pro legallyFinding stuff inside CanvaCanva ShortcutsHow to make GIF animations with CanvaUseful resources and their efficient use. And more...

www.ingramcontent.com/pod-product-compliance
Lightning Source LLC
Chambersburg PA
CBHW021142070326
40689CB00043B/999